Wartime Memories
Stories of the Second World War in the North East

by Andrew Clark

Introduction

I would like to thank all those people who have contributed their wartime memories to this book. Although the Second World War ended over seventy years ago, many of our storytellers have vivid recollections of their experiences of evacuation, the Home Guard, air raids, rationing or VE Day. Many of those sharing their memories were children at the time of the war but the fact that they were a part – in their own small way – of global events has made a lasting impression on them. It has been a pleasure to listen to their stories and record them for the book.

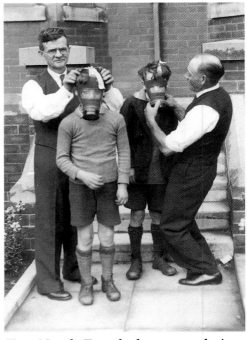

Alongside people's memories, there are also unique old photographs as well as wartime memorabilia that many will remember – Identity Cards, Ration Books, Propaganda Posters and Public Information Leaflets. These documents give first-hand information available at the time of the war and are an insight into the lives of people in the 1930s and '40s.

Over the years I have asked many people: 'What did you do in the war?' and included in the book are some of their memories. Unfortunately, I do not know the names of all of these storytellers. Please contact me if you recognise your story and I will include your name in future editions. Also I would like to hear from anyone who would like to share their experiences of the war – it's important that these memories are not forgotten and are passed on to future generations.

Andrew Clark
Summerhill Books, 2016

Two North East lads try on their gas masks.

Previous page: Dressing up time for Jean and Dick Sewell, outside 13 Bertha Street, Ferryhill, County Durham. They are in their Uncle Jack Gramsby's uniform on one of the rare occasions he was home on leave from the war.

Summerhill Books

Summerhill Books publishes North East local history books. To receive a catalogue of our titles, send a stamped addressed envelope to:

Andrew Clark, Summerhill Books, PO Box 1210, Newcastle-upon-Tyne NE99 4AH

or email: summerhillbooks@yahoo.co.uk

or visit our website to view our full range of books: **www.summerhillbooks.co.uk**

Copyright Andrew Clark 2016

First published in 2012
Revised and reprinted in 2016 by

Summerhill Books
PO Box 1210, Newcastle-upon-Tyne NE99 4AH

www.summerhillbooks.co.uk

email: summerhillbooks@yahoo.co.uk

ISBN: 978-1-906721-47-3

Contents

Two wartime posters with slogans that are still remembered today – 'Careless Talk Costs Lives' and 'Coughs and Sneezes Spread Diseases'.

War Is Declared

Left: Sandbags in front of the Ear, Nose and Throat Hospital, Newcastle, in 1938. War was thought to be imminent at this time because of Adolf Hitler's aggressive policies towards neighbouring countries. Preparations for war were made and many public buildings had sandbags placed outside of them. Gas masks were issued and volunteers joined the ARP. Prime Minister, Neville Chamberlain met with Hitler in Munich for talks and came back to Britain to declare: 'Peace in our Time' (*below*).

Chamberlain had agreed to Germany taking over part of Czechoslovakia and it was hoped this would be the end of Hitler's expansionist plans. However, peace was to last less than a year when war was declared after Germany invaded Poland.

The main form of mass communication before the Second World War was the radio – or wireless as most people called it. People crowded round the wireless on Sunday, 3rd September 1939 to hear Neville Chamberlain make this announcement:

'This morning the British Ambassador in Berlin handed the German Government a final note, stating that, unless we heard from them by 11 o'clock that they were prepared at once to withdraw their troops from Poland, a state of war would exist between us. I have to tell you now that no such undertaking has been received and that consequently this country is at war with Germany.'

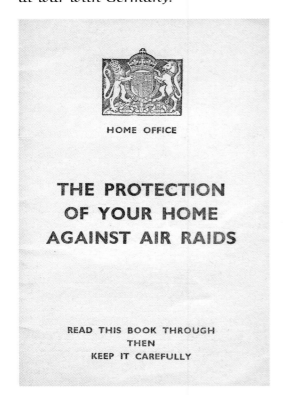

HOME OFFICE

THE PROTECTION OF YOUR HOME AGAINST AIR RAIDS

READ THIS BOOK THROUGH
THEN
KEEP IT CAREFULLY

Across the country, straight after Chamberlain had made his speech declaring war, air raid sirens sounded. This created panic in parts of the North East and some people recall being terrified. Younger children thought the sound of the sirens meant the Germans were coming straight away.

The preparations for war now increased. Air raid shelters were built and children, pregnant women and the disabled were evacuated from towns and cities.

The first year of hostilities was known as the 'Phoney War'. Little seemed to be happening and the preparations were thought to have been wasted. However, once Germany invaded the Low Countries and then France surrendered, Britain faced the threat of invasion. The Battle of Britain was to follow and the country was engulfed in all-out war with bombings, the black-out and rationing.

Left: The cover of a Home Office booklet called *The Protection of Your Home Against Air Raids*. Dozens of booklets of this type were produced by the Home Office, Ministry of Home Security, Ministry of Information and Ministry of Food to inform the public of how to cope during the war.

When Germany Invaded Poland
by Lorna Windham

The *Pilsudski*, a prestigious ship named after a famous Polish general, was a 14,294 ton twin-screw Polish liner built in Italy in 1935 to carry wealthy passengers between Poland and New York. With her measurements of 526 ft by 70 ft and 2516 hp diesel engines, a swimming pool, gym, fencing area, tennis courts, library, gift shop and decorations by contemporary Polish artists, she was considered the height of luxury at the time.

The Polish liner Pilsudski.

Germany invaded Poland on Friday, 1st September 1939 and on the following Sunday, my father, Jim Windham, at that time a 19-year-old Jarrow postman, huddled round the wireless with his family at 14, St Paul's Road, Jarrow and listened with growing concern as Prime Minister Neville Chamberlain informed the nation that Great Britain was at war with Germany. That afternoon Jim had to work and was told to go to the Oil Wharf at Jarrow Slake (near St Paul's Monastery) to collect mail from the *Pilsudski*.

It took all afternoon and several journeys as he bundled 157 heavy bags on to a barrow, trundled it along the wharf and on to a waiting van. It was exhausting work.

The Polish sailors must have taken pity on him because he was invited aboard and offered a bowl of hot soup. It was watery, but he gratefully accepted it in the spirit it was given. As he ate he thought how sad it was for the Polish sailors, who were in a foreign port, extremely worried about their families in Poland and had no hope of getting home.

A few weeks later the *Pilsudski* sailed from Newcastle on her first journey under charter to the Royal Navy as an armed Merchant Cruiser and anchored for a few days at the mouth of the Tyne.

She carried 163 crew (seven were British sailors); an unknown number of soldiers and it's thought other

Jim Windham.

passengers. Her destination was Australia, her objective to collect troops.

Jim later heard the shocking news that the ship had been sunk when she struck a German mine at 4.30 am on Sunday, 26th November 1939 and ten crewmen were lost. Captain Mamert Stankiswicz was last off his ship and clung to a life raft before being picked up by an Allied ship. Unfortunately, he died of hypothermia in Hartlepool and is buried there.

The *Pilsudski* lies off the Yorkshire coast, near Withernsea and today divers explore the wreck. Though the *Pilsudski* is no more, Jim, served in the Middle East, became Inspector at Jarrow Post Office and was awarded the BEM (British Empire Medal) for services to the Post Office when he retired. He now lives in Milton Keynes but still has many fond memories of Tyneside.

Right: Mamert Stankiswicz – the Captain of the *Pilsudski*.

Air Raid Precautions

The Air Raid Precautions Act of 1938 empowered local councils to appoint ARP Wardens as well as set up first aid posts and ambulance services and form Auxiliary Fire Services. An ARP booklet – *The Practical Guide for the Householder and Air-Raid Warden* – listed the following potential dangers:

There are three methods which an enemy operating from a distance with high-powered, speedy bombing aeroplanes might use to terrorise our civilian population and disorganise our national services:

High Explosive Attacks, involving the use of highly destructive bombs to cause destruction, injury and loss of life.

Incendiary Attacks ie, the use of fire bombs to cause widespread fires so as to create panic and disorganise essential services, especially the ARP Organisation.

Gas Attacks, involving the release, from bombs or as spray or dangerous liquid gases, vapour gases, or poisonous smokes, intended to injure or incapacitate the public, to nullify or hamper precautions taken against (1) and (2) and to make difficult the work of rescue and first aid.

Aeroplanes flying at low altitudes may also be employed to fire from machine guns at crowds of civilians or at masses of soldiers. This method is not likely to be used, however, so long as our people are well protected by our own aircraft and our anti-aircraft batteries, because of the danger to which the attacking force is itself subjected.

During an air attack death or injury may also be caused by falling shrapnel and bullets from our own anti-aircraft guns.

In the advice above it was thought that enemy planes would not use machine guns on civilians but I have spoken to several people who were shot at. One lady from Cleadon remembers blackberry picking as a young girl when a German plane fired on her. She dropped her collecting jar and ran home, only to be told off by her mother for leaving behind the blackberries.

Andrew Clark

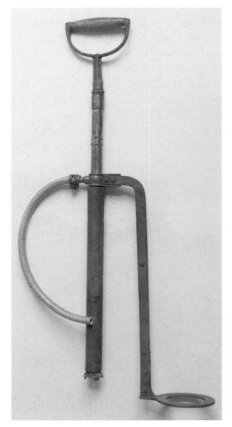

Left: A stirrup pump that was used to put out fires caused by incendiary attacks.

Below: Two ARP wardens use a stirrup pump during a practice drill in the North East.

When the ARP Units were first formed, their uniforms and equipment were quite limited and in the early part of the war consisted of a helmet, badge and armband. Eventually, uniforms were issued to all ARP Wardens, although they were basic compared with the clothes worn by the Armed Services. The cost of the early uniforms was only 11 shillings per warden.

ARP Wardens at Sacriston, County Durham. They are holding bells and rattles used to give warnings of air raids.

A rattle similar to ones used by ARP Wardens. After the war, rattles such as this were painted in football club colours and used by fans to urge on their teams.

One of the duties of the ARP Warden was to maintain the black-out so enemy planes could not be guided to their targets by any light from the ground. People lived in fear of the famous cry from the Warden – 'PUT THAT LIGHT OUT'. Persistent offenders would be fined and, in 1940, 300,000 people in Britain were prosecuted.

An advert for ARP black-out materials.

Right: Two members of Ashington Colliery ARP gas decontamination squad emerge from a shelter during a practice air raid. They are dressed in thick air-tight suits and boots. Special training was given to these squads to deal with the expected gas attacks.

An ARP Lamp with hood that directed the light of the bulb down to the ground – one of the many precautions used during the black-out

The Threat of Gas

Right: Fitting North East youngsters with gas masks at the start of the war. After gas was used during the First World War, with horrific effects, there was a real fear that the Germans would use this weapon again. Training was given to ARP Wardens on how to detect gas attacks and decontamination squads were set up to deal with clearing-up operations. Drills were carried out where the public would practice putting on their masks during mock air raids.

By 1939 over 44 million masks had been issued, however, as the war continued more and more people stopped carrying them as the threat of gas attacks did not materialise. A Government slogan at that time was: 'Take care of your gas mask and your gas mask will take care of you.'

The ARP booklet – *The Practical Guide for the Householder and Air-Raid Warden* gave this advice on the threat of Gas:

What we must know about Gas Attacks

The objects of a Gas Attack are:

1. To cause many Casualties through injury or incapacity.

2. To Disorganise Industry and Essential Services, and especially to hinder the repair and damage, and the work of rescue and first aid, necessary after high explosive attacks, it is extremely likely that an enemy attacking this country would use high explosives and gas together.

3. To Shatter the Morale of or terrorise the people.

An adult's respirator.

Hints for Householders

Always carry your respirator with you whenever you have to leave your home or place of business, and an identify label on which your name and address are clearly written.

Don't damage your gas mask by carrying it by the straps. Hold it by the canister.

Don't let the children play with their gas masks.

Don't wear glasses, or if a women, a hair net, when you have to put on your respirator.

The cover of a booklet produced by the Ministry of Home Security giving advice on anti-gas protection of babies and young children. This included instructions for use of the baby's protective helmet.

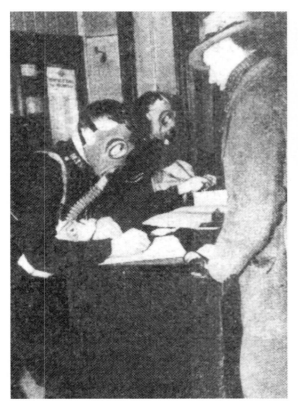

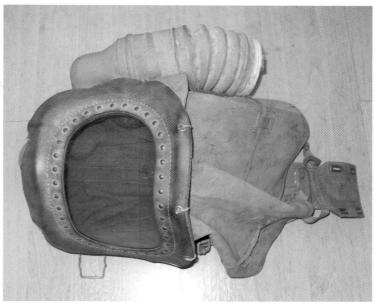

A baby's respirator or protective helmet with a hand-powered pump at the side. Adults had to be with the child at all times to pump the air. Some babies were terrified to be placed in such devices. Thankfully they were never used in a real gas attack.

Above: A 'warhorse' is fitted with a gas mask at the Royal Veterinary College in London.

Left: Policemen wearing gas masks while on duty in Middlesbrough in 1941. Even though there had been no gas attacks, practice drills were still being held all around the country, even two years into the war. In Middlesbrough at this time, the policemen wore their gas masks twice a day for 10 minutes at noon and 5 pm. It was thought to be important to set an example to the public who perhaps did not take the threat seriously.

Identity Cards

Left: Jean White showing her identification to a guard outside Vickers-Armstrong in Newcastle at 7 am, Sunday 26th May 1940. Jean was on her way into work at the engineering factory. Identity checks like this were believed to be essential to stop spies and saboteurs getting access to restricted areas.

Identity Cards had first been introduced in Britain during the First World War and were abandoned in 1919. The National Registration Act of 1939 re-introduced them and it was not until 1952 that they stopped being used. Although seen as a necessity during wartime, most people questioned their need in peacetime. It was a criminal offence not to produce a card when challenged by a police officer and when one member of the public refused to do so in 1950 it resulted in a famous civil liberties court case. The defendant lost the case but ID Cards would not survive for long. In 1952 they were scrapped and one of the reasons given was their enormous administration costs.

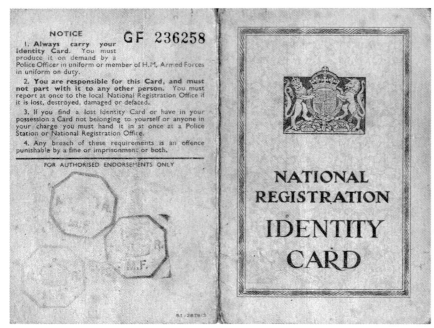

The front and back of an Identity Card. A note on the back reads:

'**Always carry your Identity Card.** You must produce it on demand by a Police Officer in uniform or member of H.M. Armed Forces in uniform on duty.'

On the inside of the card was the holder's name, address and number.

If a policeman asked for your Identity Card and you did not have it with you then you could be issued with a 'producer' (*above*). This instructed you to go to a police station and show your Identity Card within two days. Failure to do so could lead to a conviction under the National Registration Act 1939.

Gas Masks and Gun Fire
by Ann Nora Robinson (née Henderson)

As I was born in 1925 my teenage years were spent at the beginning of the Second World War. It isn't until I look back at those times that I realise how Hitler stole my youth as well as that of thousands of other teenagers throughout the world. Fortunately I can remember the good times as well as the bad and often smile at some of the incidents that happened.

One of the most important things you had to have with you at all times was your gas mask. Although you hoped you would never have to use it, you took it with you everywhere. One day I was out shopping in Fawcett Street, Sunderland, with my friend Vera Devine when Vera tripped over a gas mask. 'Someone's lost their gas mask!' exclaimed Vera and promptly kicked it into the gutter. After we had finished our shopping, which wasn't very much later as most things were rationed, we headed off back home. It was then Vera realised something was missing – it was her gas mask! We practically flew down Fawcett Street. Luckily for Vera her gas mask was still lying in the gutter where she had kicked it. But even though she never lost her gas mask again she never lived the story down.

Vera and I were practically inseparable and we often went to the pictures in our free time. We were always aware of the dangers of bombings and there was quite a bit of bomb damage in Hendon and the East End of Sunderland. So on this particular night we were on our way to The Villiers picture house (with our gas masks!), when we heard machine gun fire. We were told if ever we heard any machine gun fire to lie face down so there was less chance of being shot. When it became quiet again we continued on our way only for it to start again, so again we lay face down until it stopped. As there was little light because of the black-out we always walked close to the walls of houses. Then for the third time we heard gun fire but then it dawned on us what we thought was machine gun fire was in fact the rat-tat-tat of my belt buckle on the corrugated-iron sheeting surrounding a bombsite. When we arrived at the pictures we could not believe the state our coats were in, we were black from head to toe from diving to the ground to avoid the 'gun fire'.

Ann Nora Robinson.

The black-out came into force in Britain on 1st September 1939. Black curtains had to be hung from every window while streetlamps were put out and cars, trams and buses had their headlamps masked to reduce their glare. Accidents on the roads increased by over 100 percent and the Government produced posters that instructed people to:

Look Out in the Black-out
Until your eyes get used to the darkness
Take it easy.

Left: An advert that appeared in the *Morpeth Herald* in February 1940 that warned people of the dangers on the roads in the black-out. It says 1,200 people were killed in December alone and it gave this advice: 'Remember – if you take a chance, it may be your last!'

Air Raid Shelters and Schooldays
by Brian Scott

My mother and I shared a garden with the Burns family from the cottage next door in Wear Street, Sunderland. It wasn't much of a garden as our cottages were situated almost, but not quite, under the Queen Alexandra Bridge and the shade only allowed grass and weeds to grow.

Several months before the outbreak of war our air raid shelter was delivered and as soon as it arrived Mr Burns checked the packages thoroughly to ensure that all the parts, and all the nuts and bolts which would be required, were there. Then he set to work installing the shelter at the top of the garden well away from the bridge and the street. It would have been a long and hard tiring task if he'd been able to get on with it without interruption but because of his job he couldn't do that and the construction of the air raid shelter therefore, vital though it was to us, had to take second place.

Mr Burns' son, William, and I did what we could to help but it was very heavy work for two young lads. We were, after all, only nine or ten years old. To install the shelter it was necessary, first, to dig a hole which was approximately eleven to twelve feet long by nine or ten feet wide with a minimum depth of four feet. The shelter was more effective, however, if it was buried at a depth of five feet or more.

After the main hole was dug it was necessary to dig another hole, though nowhere near as big, to provide drainage. With the provision of the drainage pit the erection of the shelter could begin. That was where William and I were able to help by holding the sections upright and keeping them still while Mr Burns bolted them together. It wasn't long before the shelter was

Soil is placed over an Anderson Shelter for extra protection.

erected and the task of covering it with soil and rubble could begin. Even when that task was completed, however, the shelter was far from ready for use. Some sort of bedding or seating had to be installed along with some form of heating.

I must give Mr Burns credit – after his daily work he toiled long and hard and valiantly to install the shelter and to make it cosy and comfortable as he possibly could. No one knew for how long or how often the air raid shelters would be used. On Friday the first day of September, two days before the outbreak of the war, Mr Burns, to his great relief, declared that our air raid shelter was complete and that there was no more he could do to it. His handiwork was duly inspected by Mrs Burns and by my mother, both ladies declaring their entire satisfaction with it.

Then at 11 am on the 3rd September we listened to Neville Chamberlain's speech on the wireless. It seemed that, after the speech, everyone living in the street came outside to discuss the gravity of what they had just heard. Some played it down saying that even at that late hour Nazi Germany would back down. Others, more gloomily, forecast that the war would last for two, or three, or five or, even ten years. No one, as far as I recall, ever suggested that we would lose the war. It was just a question of how long it would take us to beat the enemy. At about half past eleven, just when the debates were heating up, there sounded the first air raid warning alarm of the war. With mixed feelings people stood and gazed at each other. Some cried, others consoled them. Most people were too stunned to do anything. But one man in our street neither cried nor consoled nor was he stunned by the turn of events. As the sirens wailed Mr Burns was cajoling, ordering, demanding, that we take our places in the shelter. By the time that he had convinced us that the shelter was the best, and safest, place for us to be, it was too late. The 'all clear' was sounding and the 'air raid' was over.

Many school teachers volunteered for service in the Armed Forces, but it wasn't only the shortage of teachers which created problems. Many of the schools were needed for the distribution of ration books and gas masks and for the provision of rest centres for the homeless in the event of air raids and the consequent mass destruction of homes. The initial response to the shortage of teachers and the possible loss, however temporary, of premises was the introduction of part-time education. Whilst not the ideal solution it did provide continuity of a sort until such times as the situation became clearer and longer term plans could be made and carried out. Premises suitable for use as classrooms were sought after. Church halls, factories with spare rooms, empty shops or houses, were commandeered and adapted to schoolroom use. In my own case the classroom to which I was allocated was a large garden shed on a piece of land at the top of Wear Street. Each classroom had to serve all ages within a certain district. It is a credit to the quality of the teaching staff that, despite all these difficulties, standards remained so very high.

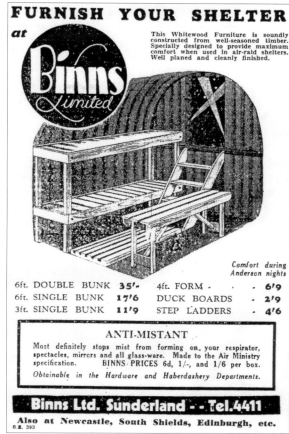

An advert from the department store Binns for furnishing your shelter.

Mr Mountain is the only teacher I can remember during those first very difficult months of the war. He was an elderly gentleman who, but for the outbreak of the war, would probably have gone into well-earned retirement. His patience with us was remarkable. You must remember that the difficulties were not only with the Education Authorities and the teachers. The pupils were also suffering from the disruptions and tragedies of war. Many of us had seen our brothers and fathers and uncles and cousins called up to war service. Many of us were under stress at home due to mothers being on war work and at the same time many of us were under stress to do well in examinations, so that we could go to the Grammar School. Mr Mountain not only continued to teach us to his own high standard but he was able to guide us, to soothe us, to calm our fears, to be a sort of father figure to us all as well as being our teacher and friend. In due time I sat and passed my exams with a result which entitled me to a place at Monkwearmouth Central School. Soon I left that hut and went on to the new school and I heard no more about Mr Mountain. My schooling was now more settled but there were still times when, because of air raids, it was interrupted.

'Don't dance about on it, Winnie, you might fall through.'

A cartoon from Punch looks at the funny side of the Anderson Shelter.

Evacuation

Right: Children line up in a school yard and are given instructions for evacuation. They have labels around their necks which would have on it their name and perhaps their school. Their clothes and a few belongings are in a mixture of suitcases, pillow cases or brown paper parcels. They are also carrying their gas masks. Mothers were often given a list of items the children would need while they were away. Most evacuations were organised by schools with teachers putting the pupils on the trains or buses that would take them to the countryside and safety. Teachers then stayed in the same area as the children and temporary schools were set up to continue their education.

Operation Pied Piper

When the war started it was expected that towns and cities would soon be heavily bombed and there would be thousand of casualties. The Government immediately organised 'Operation Pied Piper' – the perfect title for an operation that was to take away the children from the threatened danger. As well as children, evacuees included pregnant mothers and the disabled.

It was not compulsory for parents to send their children to the country but most families thought it was best that they went. Families who took in children were given a small payment to help pay for food and other expenses. It was illegal for someone to refuse to take in an evacuee.

Children from Newcastle were mostly sent to what is now Cumbria; Wallsend and North Shields children went to Northumberland; while those from Gateshead, South Shields and Sunderland were evacuated to safer parts of County Durham and Yorkshire.

Can you imagine today giving up your children to complete strangers – possibly for years? The evacuees were often taken to a church or village hall where they would be picked out by families who would take them home. It is said that bonnie bairns would be picked first or a strong lad if there was work to be done. If a family had all lads they might want a girl or if there was all girls at home they would pick a boy. One man from Gateshead told me about his experiences of being evacuated to the country. Him and all of his school friends were taken by bus to a village in County Durham and he remembers all the farmers were waiting for the evacuees to arrive. As they got off the bus they picked all the big lads for work on their farms. He said it was just like they were choosing cattle at the market.

One lady from Benwell in Newcastle told me that the day she was evacuated all the children in her school were given biscuits to eat on their journey. She remembers that almost every child ate the biscuits before they even got on the bus that would take them to the Central Station in Newcastle.

Andrew Clark

An Evacuee's Story
by Eileen Hopper (née Conlin)

Imagine one day in September 1939 that your Mother told you something very important that would affect us all was on the radio and they wanted to listen to the news. Not everyone in those days had a radio so our next-door neighbour was invited in. What they heard was that our country, Britain was now at war with Germany, they were both very sad and worried about what could happen as husbands and sons would be sent away to fight in the war.

Eileen Hopper.

I was only five years old, too little to realise what this would mean, but the very next day I was sent to the country where they thought it would be safe. Sunderland where I lived was a very important shipbuilding town, then one of the biggest in the world, with oil terminals, docks, factories and gas works, just the type of place the German aeroplanes would come and bomb. My family knew a lady that had a spare room where we could stay, so with my Auntie Elsie and my three cousins, Ronnie, 9, Pat, 7, and Jean, 6, we went to Egglestone in Teesdale. Five of us were living in one bedroom in someone else's house and it was crowded. Luckily, after a while, we were able to rent part of a farmhouse up the hill where we had to walk one mile to school every day.

This house was much better really, part of a big farmhouse with more room to run about and play, but it only had three rooms, a living room, a big kitchen and one bedroom. We had no electric light, just oil lamps and candles to light us to bed. The toilet was across the farmyard and up a long garden in the pitch black. There was no mains water, it was called a dry toilet and you threw ashes on top and when our Dads came they shovelled it out a door at the back. We could go through to the farmer's part of the house by going through a big dairy along a passage. It was on a working farm belonging to Mr and Miss Busby set high on a hill overlooking lovely countryside right across the River Tees to the hills beyond. Egglestone is situated four miles from Middleton-in-Teesdale and six miles from Barnard Castle. To come on the bus our parents had to get four different buses to Durham, Bishop Auckland, Evenwood then Egglestone.

Food was very short during the war, as ships couldn't bring supplies from over the sea as they were sunk by German U-boats, so what we ate had to be grown in England. We all had ration books with so many points to spend weekly and we could only buy a small packet of sweets each week. There was horrible tiny black liquorice sweets off ration but I didn't really like them. I think they were called Nipits. At the farm we had to share what food we had as it was rationed. We were lucky on the farm as we could get eggs and milk easily. It was very hard for people thinking of nourishing and tasty food to feed their family – no ice cream, no bananas or oranges or any other fruit that grew in hot countries. Every one turned their gardens into vegetable plots so they would have more food. We would go into the pantry and look at the few tins of fruit and work out who would have what for their birthday. That is the only time we had tinned fruit, as it was hard to get, with jelly and custard. You couldn't go to a supermarket then and load up your trolley, you got a little bit of butter, sugar, tea, a small portion of meat and a few eggs but the shopkeeper took your coupon out for each week so no one could get any extra.

R.B.11 PERSONAL POINTS (SWEETS) 21

16

Food Office Code No. as on front cover [   ]

Surname and Initials...

This page may be detached and used by itself but, if you do detach it, you should fill in details above.

E6	E6	E6	E6	D6	D6	D6	D6
E5	E5	E5	E5	D5	D5	D5	D5
E4	E4	E4	E4	D4	D4	D4	D4
E3	E3	E3	E3	D3	D3	D3	D3
E2	E2	E2	E2	D2	D2	D2	D2
E1	E1	E1	E1	D1	D1	D1	D1

The personal points page for sweets from a ration book.

Obviously we were unhappy being away from our Mams and Dads but people thought you were soft if you made a fuss and called you a baby if you cried and we never told our aunties about any troubles at school. I started to wet the bed at night, which is a sign you are worried about something and I really wanted to go home.

Later another two aunts who had new babies came to look after us. Auntie Elsie was not married and had to go and work in an ammunition factory to help the soldiers who were fighting – you had no choice, either do that or join the Forces. That added another three children Rita, 2, and babies Colin and Pauline

A visit from Auntie Vera. Left to right: Jean, Eileen, Ronnie, Pat, unknown friend and Rita in front. Our part of the house was the two windows on the left and the extension.

born 1942. Auntie Ella had Colin in 1939, his father was in the Army and was fighting in France. It was a very worrying time for her as her husband was at Dunkirk, where thousands of soldiers were trapped and couldn't get back over the English Channel. Then brave people with all sorts of boats, large and small, came sailing over to help them escape from the beaches, and he then came home on leave. Auntie Vera came later with her new baby Pauline. Her home was in London, which was very badly bombed so she didn't want to take a baby there to live.

All the beds were in one upstairs room; there were three big beds and two cots with a spare folding bed downstairs. Our parents couldn't come very often, as not many people had cars and petrol was rationed. In those days, you only got one or two weeks holiday a year and they would come to visit us and take us out for days. They also tried to come for Christmas and our birthdays if they could. They had to make beds up on the floor as there was not much room, but they didn't care, as they wanted to see us so much.

The cover of a leaflet with information on how to use your gas mask.

We used to have concerts to entertain them and all learned different things to say and collect wild flower posies to give to our Mams. We always had to carry our gas masks – mine was in an Ostermilk tin painted red on a strap to go over my shoulder. I remember once going to Bowes Museum in Barnard Castle and I left my gas mask on a seat in the grounds. The next day my Dad walked there and back as the bus only ran on market day, six miles each way, and I would have got into trouble not having a gas mask. We had to have air raid practice at school, rather like fire drill, so that we would be ready to march to the school shelter in the case of an air raid.

We would wander for miles around the place. There were two woods on the farm, one called the Beech Woods, as it was all deciduous trees and one going up the hill, which were mainly pine and larch trees and our own frog pond where we would collect frog spawn. All around were the moors covered with heather with streams running across them. It was a wonderful playground and we had lots more freedom.

My Dad didn't join the Army as he worked at the Gas Works in Hendon and they needed to make the fuel to keep the homes and factories going. Certain trades like mining and shipbuilding allowed people not to join up as they were part of the war effort. In those days mothers didn't usually work but my Mam went back to work in a shop as all the young girls had joined the ATS, the WRAF or the Wrens.

We thought it was awful having to stay away from our real home, but our parents knew there were lots of houses getting bombed, people getting killed in the air raids, and wanted us to be safe from harm or maybe getting killed. I only came back to Sunderland occasionally to go to the hospital or eye infirmary for appointments. If there was an air raid we had to go in to the air raid shelter in the back yard, where there were wooden bunks and it was safer from the bombs. Because I was so young it seemed exciting. It was lovely having my Mam to myself when I came home; she did lots of special things for me because she was so pleased to have me home.

I thought it was exciting when I came home and there was an air raid. I wasn't scared because I was too young to know how dangerous it was. The air raid siren howled in the night and everyone ran for shelter. You could hear bombs dropping and see the searchlights flashing around the sky looking for German bombers and the flashes of Ack-Ack guns trying to shoot them down. When the raid was over and the planes flew back a different sort of siren went called the 'All Clear'.

Children in Sunderland couldn't go to the beach as there was rolls of barbed wire right along the front at Roker and Seaburn and parts of the sea front was only for the military. In the parks were troops of soldiers and they had laid big squares of concrete with metal hooks set in them and attached to them were barrage balloons. These were big silver balloons let into the sky to foil the planes and stop them getting over the town, there were also gun stations and searchlights in various places but well-guarded. The barrage balloons were the first thing I saw when I was coming home and I knew I was getting near Sunderland.

It was lovely countryside where we were; we could play in the woods and fields and explore the moors or wander miles away from home. Sometimes we would see lorry loads of soldiers using the moors as practice grounds and we would play with the

A visit from our Mams. Eileen with her Mam, Bessie; Rita with Ella; Pat with Lily; and Jean with Nan. Uncle Norman's car is showing.

empty cartridges on the ground. I don't think we should have done this as it was probably dangerous. I can remember having to hide in the house when English and German planes were firing at each other in the sky overhead; I think this must have been the time of the Battle of Britain. We were frightened the Germans were landing. My cousins were walking to the next village and the ARP warden told them to lie in the ditch and cover their heads with their arms for safety.

Sunderland was very badly damaged during the war, many streets had empty gaps where the houses were bombed and were left for years before new houses were built. Most of the places bombed were round the Docks area with streets of terraced houses, some of them quite old with no facilities that you take for granted such as indoor toilets and bathrooms. When these were bombed it was a good chance after the war to build new more modern houses on the edge of Sunderland and large council estates were started where they could have all mod cons as they were called.

I was at Egglestone for over four years; my cousins were like brothers and sisters to me with living together so long. I was luckier than some children who had to go and stay with strangers when they were evacuated; at least I had my family around. Eventually we all came back to Sunderland, it was a job to find a house for my aunt and her family as so many houses had been bombed. My parents' house had been damaged and the ceilings fell down but it was repaired again and it was lovely to come home. At the time I said I never wanted to go back but now when all my cousins and aunts get together we look back and talk happily about our days in Egglestone.

A War Baby
by George Laws

I was born in May 1943 and brought up in Bede Crescent, Holy Cross, Wallsend which was a separate, almost village like environment, at that time. It consisted of only seven streets, a cemetery and fields. My father was Cuthbert Laws who was a turner/brass finisher (a Reserved Occupation) in the shipyards and engineering works of the Tyne. My mother was Lilian Laws (previously Wade, née Daley) who was a widow with two daughters when my father married her. Her previous husband having been killed in a road accident whilst cycling to work at the Rising Sun Colliery.

My earliest recollections are of being told by my mother: 'You had a good start in life as you were born in a mansion!' She was referring to Stagshaw House, Corbridge, as this was used as a temporary Emergency Maternity Hospital during the Second World War.

George Laws.

A letter addressed to 'Mrs Lilian Laws, c/o Stagshaw House, Emergency Maternity Hospital, Corbridge on Tyne.'

My mother, like many wartime mums, was evacuated to Stagshaw House. I believe that the mothers stayed at Stagshaw for about 10 days after giving birth as was the custom in those days, before returning to their homes. I have an envelope addressed to her at Stagshaw House. Also my Birth Certificate states in the 'When and Where Born Section': 'Twenty fourth May 1943 Stagshaw House.'

We had relatives who lived at Corbridge and when we went to visit them my mother used to make jokes about taking me home. She would point out the large mansion on the hillside and say: 'That's your birthplace son.'

This always aroused curiosity in me and in later years I travelled along the A69 and drove past Corbridge on the way to Fallowfield Dene at Acomb – a popular weekend caravanning place for my wife and kids. I can't remember what the occasion was but one weekend we spotted notices for an open day at Stagshaw House and took the opportunity of visiting my birthplace. Whilst looking around the grounds, I met the 'Lady of the House' who was most interested to hear of my story, and said that she had been pleased to meet a number of other people with the same start in life.

The owners of Stagshaw House were, and may well still be, the Straker Family. Strakers used to be a large Motor Dealership in Newcastle for Morris cars, this was situated on the south corner of Market Street and Carliol Street, and one of the most prominent and well-respected businesses in town.

George with his parents, Cuthbert and Lilian Laws.

George Laws with his grandparents, James and Mary Jane Douglass.

Bomb damage behind George's grandparents' house in Bede Crescent, Holy Cross, Wallsend.

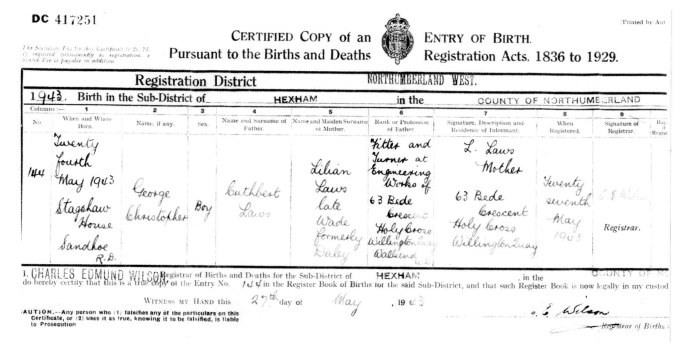

George's birth certificate, showing he was born in Stagshaw House.

A Sad Evacuee's Story

Most people speak in a very positive way about their experiences as an evacuee. However, one lady from Newcastle had an upsetting story to tell of when she was young. She was from Scotswood and remembers the chaos at the local station with too many children and not enough adults to keep order. Some of the children were very young and didn't understand what was going on and why they were being taken away from their parents. Young children were crying and it was very difficult to comfort them. The evacuees were taken to Cumbria by train and taken to a church hall where local families were waiting to take them in. All of the children were chosen until there was only one child left – the young girl from Scotswood – and she was not picked by any of the families. Sixty years later she still remembers how upsetting this was. An adult took her around the village in the dark and knocked on doors until someone would take her. How upsetting this must have been for a young child – something she never forgot.

Andrew Clark

Rationing

Ration books were first issued in January 1940 and became part of life in Britain until the 1950s. After the war some rations were further reduced and bread was first rationed in 1946.

Below is a list of some of the items that were rationed:

	First Rationed	De-Rationed
Tea	1940	1952
Sugar	1940	1953
Butter	1940	1954
Meat	1940	1954
Petrol	1940	1950
Eggs	1941	1953
Cheese	1941	1954
Clothes	1941	1949
Jam	1941	1948
Sweets	1942	1953
Bread	1946	1948

Right: A Ministry of Food ration book from 1953-54 when rationing finally ended. A lot of people kept their last ration books – perhaps they thought rationing would return!

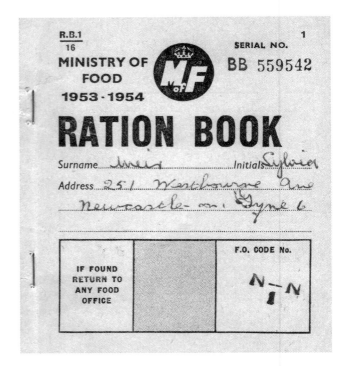

Yes We Have No Bananas … We Have No Bananas Today

The words of this popular song were written in the 1920s but it was often heard during the war when bananas became so scarce. For the majority of the war it was almost impossible to buy them and the few that were seen would often be brought from oversees by men in the Navy.

People remember the first time they saw a banana and a common reaction was to try to eat it without taking off the skin. Not everyone knew they had to be peeled. Even peeling one was a problem for some. Having never seen a banana peeled before, some attempts included trying to squeeze the fruit from its skin hoping it would pop out.

One popular wartime recipe was thought to be a good replacement for the lack of bananas. The idea was to boil parsnips – that looked a little like bananas and were easily obtained – until all their taste was gone. Then banana essence was added. Some enjoyed the taste while others thought it was horrible. The best way to eat it was to mash it all up and add some sugar.

The parsnip and the banana.

Queuing For Bananas

It was said that when there was rationing, if you saw a queue you joined it. There must be a reason why everyone else was queuing.

I once gave a talk to a ladies group in Easington in County Durham and everyone of them could remember when bananas first went on sale in the village after the war. The queue stretched out of the shop and down the street for the fruit. When you got to the front it was one banana per customer.

A lady in Benwell, Newcastle, told me she also queued up at a greengrocers after the war but she had no money – she just wanted to have a look at a banana.

Andrew Clark

A Present From Overseas

A gentleman from Boldon in South Tyneside told me about the first time he saw a banana. He was a young boy when the war ended and had up to then never seen a one. A relation in the Navy was bringing back some bananas and the lad was told by his family if he was a good boy that week he would be given one. So at the end of the week, when he had been good, he sat at the kitchen table with his whole family watching him eat his present.

Before him was a black object. The banana had taken so long to get to Britain it had become ripe and dark. 'Weren't they supposed to be yellow?' he thought. With his family watching him he took one bit of this ripe banana and immediately spat it out – it was revolting!

Oranges From America

A lady from South Shields remembered the time she saw her first orange during the war. She was travelling on a train from the South of England and in their carriage were some American soldiers. They had their kit bags with them and one of the soldiers got some oranges out of his bag. Word quickly went round the train that the Americans had this precious fruit. The soldiers realised the fuss their oranges had caused and to their credit they went up and down the train offering segments to the other passengers. At that time oranges were limited in Britain to pregnant mothers and so this was a rare treat for everyone on the train.

Andrew Clark

Save Bread and You Save Lives

Although bread was not rationed until 1946, it was seen as an important commodity during wartime. Wheat had to be imported from abroad and, with so many ships being sunk by German U-boats, the humble loaf was seen as an expensive luxury. *Below*: A wartime poster with a loaf of bread lost at sea after a ship has been sunk.

Potato Pete

Potato Pete was a cartoon character who encouraged people to use potatoes as much as possible. Here was his song:

Potatoes new, potatoes old
Potatoes in a salad cold
Potatoes baked or mashed or fried
Potatoes whole, potatoes pied
Enjoy them all, including chips
Remember spuds don't come in ships

Another cartoon character was Clara Carrot who promoted the use of that vegetable.

Kitchen Front and Dig For Victory Week

In August 1941 Sunderland Council organised a Kitchen Front and Dig For Victory Week. It was the first major town in the North East to host such an event. The week had four aims:

1. To educate the population on how to conserve food.
2. To demonstrate how to eliminate waste while cooking.
3. To encourage the collection of waste and scrap.
4. To promote the use of land for growing vegetables.

Right: The cover of the week's official programme and recipe book. Price – one penny.

The housewife had to be very creative during the war with so many shortages and here are a few ideas from this wartime recipe book:

Straight from the Garden Soup, Cabbage Soup, Potato and Kipper Pie, Herring and Tomato Casserole, Fatless Pastry, Economical Mince, Savoury Roly Poly, Oatmeal Supper Dish, Rabbit Mould, Stuffed Vegetable Marrow, Rook & Crow Pie, Summer Vegetable Hot Pot, Eggless Yorkshire Pudding and Chocolate Potato Cake.

With meat on the ration, butchers would offer the likes of: trotters, tripe, whale meat, rabbit, liver, kidney, black pudding, sheep's heart and even horse meat. Although some of these are still eaten today not many would have whale or horse meat on their shopping list.

Left: A window display highlighting the County Durham Garden Produce Committee 'Grow More Food' Campaign. Posters in the window include the slogans 'Dig For Victory' as well as one that says: 'Don't let Hitler stuff you – Grow your own'.

The Squander Bug

A series of propaganda posters were produced featuring the Squander Bug. This was a bug covered in swastikas who encouraged the shopper to spend too much money. At this time every effort was made not to waste precious resources and the campaign was to prevent shopping for goods you did not need or that were overpriced. The slogan was 'Don't Take the Squander Bug when you go shopping.'

A wanted poster was produced saying the Squander Bug, alias Hitler's Pal, was wanted for the crime of 'Shoppers Disease'.

Clothing Coupons

On 1st June 1941 clothes rationing was introduced. In the first year every man, women and child was allowed 66 coupons for their clothes, however, this amount varied throughout the war. Here are some items and the coupons needed to buy them in 1941:

Men and Boys

	Adult	Child
Overcoat	16	11
Coat or jacket	13	8
Trousers	8	6
Shorts	5	3
Overalls	6	4
Shirt	8	6
Pants or vest	4	2
Socks	3	1
Tie	1	1
Scarf or gloves	2	2
Boots or shoes	7	3
Dressing gown	8	6
Pyjamas	8	6

Women and Girls

	Adult	Child
Coat (over 28 in long)	14	11
Coat (under 28 in long)	11	8
Dress – woolen	11	8
Dress – other material	7	5
Blouse, cardigan, jumper	5	3
Skirt	7	5
Apron or pinafore	3	2
Pyjamas	8	6
Nightdress	6	5
Pair of stockings	2	1
Boots, shoes, slippers	5	3
Undergarments including corsets	3	2

Make Do And Mend

Right: The front cover of the Ministry of Information's 'Make Do and Mend' booklet promoting ways of saving money on clothes. Inside were some tips:

Sewing Classes
Why not join a sewing class and learn to sew? Your local Evening Institute, Technical College, or Women's Organisation is probably running a class now. Ask the Citizen Advice Bureau: they will be able to tell you when these classes meet.

Children's shoe and clothing exchanges
Make use of the children's shoe and clothing exchanges which are opening in many parts of the country. Perhaps there is one in your district: it is worth while finding out.

Advice Centres
Many advice centres are opening where you can take your worn out clothes to get advice on renovating and mending.

Mending Groups
Can you help others – for instance, by organising a group of women with some needlework skill and a little time, to repair the overalls of the local war workers? Ask the welfare or personnel departments of the factories if you can help.

An advert for John Moses, Grainger Street, Newcastle from 1942 encouraging people to knit to help with the war effort. Knitting groups were formed throughout the North East with many producing socks, gloves, scarves and balaclava helmets for the Armed Forces.

The Home Guard

In May 1940 the Local Defence Volunteers (LDV) was formed. Men quickly signed up for this new force but at first training and equipment was very basic and in short supply. Uniforms were sometimes just an armband with the letters LDV and broom handles were used until rifles became available. Even the armbands were useless when Winston Churchill made the decision to change the force's name to the Home Guard. Most members were men too old to be called up for the regular forces and who had served in the First World War. While others were workers from reserved occupations. In December 1944 the Home Guard was stood down when the threat of invasion was over.

A Home Guard unit outside Willington Parish Hall, Wallsend.

Left: Members of the York Home Guard with a captured 'enemy' Bren Gun Carrier during 'Exercise Bovril' in York in 1942. The enemy had been regular Army troops who had been ambushed by the Home Guard who made them surrender by attacking them with their rifle butts. In the foreground is seventeen-year-old Jim Pace who later became a headmaster, author and local historian in Silksworth, County Durham. He is wearing a bandage after splitting his head open on a spiked railing in the black-out.

Just Like Dad's Army
by Tom Peacock

In 1942, when I was eighteen, I joined the Home Guard based at the Team Valley Trading Estate. Later when I watched Dad's Army on television I thought just how similar the exploits of the comedy series were to my experiences in the Home Guard.

We had a lieutenant who was very proud of the fact he was an officer. He did some horrendous things. I can remember when we were marching along the Team Valley and he called 'Left Turn!' We all turned left while he turned right.

One night we went out on manoeuvres. Two men were sent on to the nearby Ravensworth Estate which was quite wooded. The platoon had to go out and search for them but they were never found and we returned to the Team Valley. After over an hour the two men came back. The lieutenant turned to one of the men and said, 'Right then, private I want you to report on what you heard while you were in the woods.'

He said: 'Well Sir, I heard nothing except the twittering of birds in the trees and the twittering of the Colonel laughing in the background.'

That was his full report. It was like something Pike would have said in Dad's Army.

I later transferred from the Team Valley to the Westerhope Home Guard and saw some strange things there as well. One time we dug up a tennis court behind the Methodist Church in Westerhope so we could dig trenches to defend ourselves if Britain was invaded. We completely destroyed that tennis court for nothing because if the Germans did come those trenches would have been in the wrong place. How could we defend the village from the back of the church?

My brother, Stan, was also in the Westerhope Home Guard and on one occasion we were cleaning our rifles at home. We were fortunate to have rifles as in the early

Westerhope Home Guard in front of the Orion Picture House in the village, around 1941 – just before Tom Peacock joined them.

stages of the war the Home Guard used broomsticks to practice for drill. A 'pull-through' was used to keep the barrel of your rifle clean. This was a metal rod with a cord on the end and you pushed this through. We got the pull-through stuck and it wouldn't budge. I suggested to Stan that he pulled the rifle while I stood on the cord. Stan pulled and sure enough it came away but it shot out of the rifle and smashed a light fitting that my parents had since they were married – it was absolutely shattered. What a disaster!

Stan and I were out on manoeuvres in Newbiggin Hall and we were instructed to follow some men who were the 'enemy'. We were supposed to follow them from a distance so we could report on their movements. At one point we were crawling alongside a hedge when we came across some other men and continued crawling along with them. Suddenly I realised we were crawling alongside the 'enemy'.

One of the weapons we used was an EY Discharger. This was a standard rifle with a cup at the end in which you placed a Mills bomb. When you discharged the rifle the bomb flew out. One day when the platoon was on manoeuvres we were practising firing the EY Discharger. When it came to my turn, I fired and the rifle butt fell off completely. What would have happened if we had ever been in wartime conditions, I just don't know.

Air Raids

Right: A Heinkel bomber over North Seaton, near Ashington in 1941.

After the so-called phoney war of 1939, the fall of France in 1940 was followed by the Battle of Britain. Bombing raids became more common and the industry of Tyneside and Wearside became prime targets. Local people watched enemy planes in the sky and also saw the occasional dogfight when British Hurricanes or Spitfires engaged the enemy. Night-time brought the black-out, searchlights and the sound of anti-aircraft guns as well as sleeping in Anderson and Morrison Shelters.

Left: A reconnaissance photograph of Sunderland taken by a German plane a few weeks before the start of the war. Marked on the photo are four targets:

A. Greenwell's ship repair yard.

B. Hudson's Dock

C. Thompson's shipyard

D. Austin's shipyard

Sunderland had severe air raids from 1940 to 1943 and the Luftwaffe hit all four of its targets. The Germans' aim was to disrupt the shipbuilding industry on the Wear, however, they did not stop the town producing a record number of ships.

Sunderland suffered extensive damage during the war and was the most bombed town in the North East – the seventh most bombed in the country. However, the North East did not see the more severe bombing blitz that was witnessed in London, Hull and Coventry.

St George's Road, Cullercoats, probably after the raid on 11th/12th October 1942 when six people were killed. The family in the foreground load a few possessions on to a cart. Other pieces of furniture stand nearby.

Protection for civilians from bombs was basic but effective. Many families had Anderson Shelters in their gardens – named after Sir John Anderson who was responsible for air raid precautions before the war. If you did not have a garden, a brick shelter could be built and some remained in back yards in areas of Newcastle such as Byker and Benwell well after the war. The Morrison Shelter – named after Herbert Morrison, Minister for Home Security – was designed for inside the house and was a table structure with a cage underneath. Indoor alternatives to the Morrison Shelter were to go under the stairs or in the cellar if you had one. Most people, before they entered their shelter, had ready a case with all their most important items in it – such as insurance documents, ration books and money. All of these would be essential if you were bombed-out.

Liver and Bombs

I was giving a wartime talk in South Shields when one man recalled this memory from when he was a boy in nearby Boldon Colliery. One day he was at home in the kitchen with his mam waiting for his dad to come in from work from the nearby colliery. Like many pitmen's wives, his mother was busy making her husband's tea so it would be ready for him when he got home. On this particular day his mam was cooking some liver. Just as his dad got home a bomb dropped nearby. There had been no warning or time for the siren to sound. The bomb was probably from a lone German plane that may have been returning back to the continent from a mission and was releasing the last of its load. The force of the explosion blew off their back door and the pitman instinctively dived on top of his wife and son to protect them. Fortunately, none of them were hurt but their house was a mess. There was debris everywhere and soot had come down the chimney covering most of the room. When the dust had settled his mam went looking for the liver. It was found covered in soot and she started trying to clean it. She turned to her husband and said, 'You're still going to eat it. I'll not see it go to waste!'

Andrew Clark

A crowd of people on a North East bombsite. The children seem particularly interested in what is happening. For many young people the war must have been an exciting time – they left the worrying for their parents. Many schools were closed on a morning if an air raid went on till late in the night and that was good news for the children who wanted time off to explore the bomb craters that now became their playgrounds. A favourite hobby at that time was to collect shrapnel and perhaps swap some good bits with your school friends.

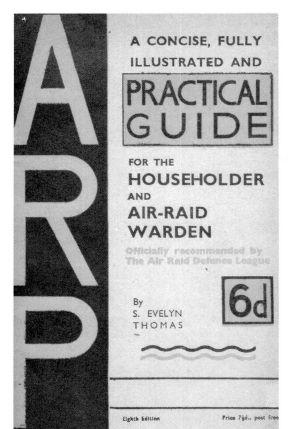

A CONCISE, FULLY ILLUSTRATED AND **PRACTICAL GUIDE** FOR THE HOUSEHOLDER AND AIR-RAID WARDEN

Officially recommended by The Air Raid Defence League

By S. EVELYN THOMAS

6d

Eighth Edition   Price 7½d., post free

Air Raid Drills

Children who weren't evacuated would take part in air raid drills at school. While I was giving a talk to Blyth History Society, one of the members recalled one of these drills.

As a child she wore the small tacks on the soles of her shoes called 'segs' that helped protect the shoe from wear. These segs made a noise when the children were marched across the school yard and into the shelter. She was told to be quiet by her teacher.

'Why, is Hitler listening?' she replied.

Andrew Clark

Left: The ARP booklet – *The Practical Guide for the Householder and Air-Raid Warden.* The booklet includes a section of hints for householders during a raid. The first words of that section are: 'Keep calm. Don't panic.'

The devastation after a direct hit on a communal shelter that was below the Wilkinson's Lemonade Factory, on the corner of George Street and King Street in North Shields, on 3rd May 1941. One hundred and seven people were killed in the worst bombing incident in the North East during the war.

King George VI and Queen Elizabeth visit a bomb damaged area in Sunderland. The King and Queen made several morale-boosting visits to the North East. The Royal family lived through the dangers of the Blitz as all Londoners did. When bombs exploded in Buckingham Palace courtyard the Queen said: 'I am glad we have been bombed. It makes me feel we can look the East End in the face.'

Bombs on Leave
by Lorna Windham

It was 9th April 1941. Jim Windham was a gunner in the Royal Artillery looking forward to a few days leave from where he'd been training with broom handles (there were no rifles) at Jersey Marine, Swansea. When travelling home by the last train from Newcastle to Jarrow, he wearily learned the line had been bombed and that he had to get off at Pelaw.

A bus dropped him at the Ben Lomond Hotel in Jarrow. All he could see were the beams of searchlights as the boom of anti-aircraft guns reverberated in his ears. He'd arrived in the middle of a bombing raid!

Concerned about his family in their terraced flat not far from the Tyne, he set off at a fast pace for St Paul's Road and heard a tremendous crash as a landmine fell on Sheldon Street. There was another crash behind him which he thought had blown in the windows of the Station Hotel.

Another bomb missed oil tanks by about 100 yards creating a huge crater in the road at the bottom of Church Bank (near St Paul's Monastery) and preventing buses going to and from Jarrow.

It was with great relief that he found the flat standing and his family alive. The raid lasted for four hours starting at 11.25 pm. Bombs hit the Gas and Water Works and incendiaries fell like rain. Clyde Street lost its windows and ceilings and a bomb fell behind Beech Terrace. It was only later that he discovered that thirty people had died in Sheldon Street.

He often thinks back to that night and wryly remembers how he'd been looking forward to a quiet time with his family but arrived in the middle of a bombardment.

Jim Windham.

Stories of the Shelters

A lady in Newcastle told me the story of one air raid she could remember. She was a young girl, living with her mother and grandmother. When the siren sounded, her grandmother was always reluctant to get out of bed and go downstairs to the Anderson Shelter in the garden.

One particular night all the family were shouting to their nana to hurry up. They were all in the shelter but were waiting for her.

'Hurry up. You need to come downstairs,' they cried.

'I'm looking for my false teeth,' she shouted back.

'What do you want your teeth for?' replied her daughter. 'They're dropping bombs not sandwiches.'

I heard another story while I was working on a history project in a school in North Shields where a number of local people were invited to share their memories of the war. You could hear a pin drop as the children listened to these stories as they were so enthralled. My favourite was when one person recalled that their dog was always the first in the shelter, even before the siren had sounded. As soon as the dog ran to the shelter all the family knew a raid was imminent and got prepared. As dogs have much better hearing than humans it must have been able to hear the danger before anyone else.

When I told this story in Gateshead a lady said her dog did exactly the same thing. Then a lady from Newcastle told me her dog would bark non-stop during an air raid.

Andrew Clark

Parachute Mine and Prayers
by Maisie Tait Cuthbertson

When the landmine fell on Lynemouth on 14th February 1941 I was nearly four years old. My Aunt Meggie and Uncle Will, and cousins Bill and Raymond Tait, lived in No 49 Dalton Avenue near to the blast. Aunt Meggie, who was out of bed, was buried under the rubble of the house and was only rescued because her hand was seen sticking out. Uncle Will, who was in bed, ended up with his head stuck through the bars of the brass bed head. Our Bill had the presence of mind to tear up bedsheets and wrap his and brother Raymond's feet in them which meant they could pick their way outside through the glass and debris. They managed to reach our house at 6 Bridge Road, cut, bruised and covered in thick dust. They were taken in, comforted, bathed and my granddad's shirts served as nightwear. Uncle Will also came later that night after being rescued but I believe Aunt Meggie had still not been found so it was a worrying time for everyone.

The family stayed with us for a short while before being rehoused and I can remember my cousins and me taking shelter in a cupboard in an alcove next to the fireplace when the German planes were flying over. Mam would sit on the cracket with her head inside the cupboard to comfort the three of us. My granddad, Bob Tait, kept pails of sand in the toilet downstairs in readiness for any incendiary or shrapnel fires and on one occasion we had six fires which left holes in our lawn. To me at four years old this was an exciting adventure and, having my cousins stay with us, I do not remember being afraid. Grandma Dorothy was a Methodist lay preacher and had great faith that we would be all right. She refused to take shelter during an air raid warning and would sit in her rocking chair while the planes buzzed overhead rocking and praying that, 'The Lord will provide'. He did and we survived.

Maisie's grandfather in the bomb crater at Lynemouth.

The aftermath of the bombing at Lynemouth. Sadly, one woman, Mrs Leonora Athey, was killed – her home was in Dalton Avenue near the explosion. Seventy-four people were injured, mainly by flying glass.

Watching the Battle of Britain
by George Forster

I can see our family now sitting around the radio listening intently to the speeches of Winston Churchill. There would be complete silence and I found myself mesmerised by his voice. After Dunkirk, and the miracle of getting so many of our soldiers back home, his speeches meant so much to us. I can remember seeing the wounded and tired troops from Dunkirk on trains going North and giving them a cheer and a wave.

George Forster.

Then Hermann Goering unleashed his Luftwaffe and the residents of my hometown of Seaham suffered from Dorniers and Heinkels. One day, when the Battle of Britain was at its height, I stood on the workbench in our back yard watching the swirling vapour trails almost all around. I saw a German plane going seaward with a Hurricane (or was it a Spitfire) on its tail. It was losing height and then went out of sight. We heard later that survivors had been picked up from the sea and brought ashore to be taken away as POWs but first had to be protected from attack by angry residents.

My father was so proud of our garden that he refused to break up the carefully laid concrete paths to accommodate an air raid shelter but we were able to share the Hudson's next door. My brother and I would dread the noise of sirens and having to get out of our warm bed and on the odd occasion we would refuse. But there was a time when we were pleased to have heeded our parent's warning. One night the bombing had been severe and close. When we returned to our house after the all-clear was sounded, we found most of our ceiling was down. A huge slab of ceiling lay across our bed which could have killed us.

I was home one day with my mother when we heard the drone of a lone aircraft – a Dornier 217 I believe. I dashed outside and stood on my father's workbench with a sieve on my head. I ignored my mother's screams for me to get indoors and under the table. I watched as two objects left the plane, which I thought at first were parachutists, but they did not open. There was the sound of 'wheee' then a 'pop'. About a minute later I jumped down from the bench, opened the back gate and was then enveloped in a cloud of dust. Later we learned that two landmines had been dropped on Viceroy Street killing several people.

An unexploded German bomb that fell on the Newcastle.

There was another time when I witnessed a landmine on a chute hanging from a tree on the road to Dalton-le-Dale. I don't know how this was dealt with.

This was an age when most of us had bogies – a contraption of four wheels fixed to a plank with a box to sit on and a rope to turn the front wheels for steerage. We would take these all round the shops in Seaham collecting cardboard and paper for the war effort. I remember a bring and buy sale with goods on clippy mats outside our back door – the money raised going to the Spitfire Fund. If my memory serves me right it cost £6,000 to buy a Spitfire.

During the war I was in the Air Training Corps but by the time I was old enough I went into the Army and by the time I'd finished training it was VE Day. I did think I would still be fighting in the Far East but then Japan surrendered.

I Wasn't Allowed to Join the RAF
by Tom Peacock

I was at home with my parents when war was declared. I was fifteen years old at the time. Everyone anticipated that the announcement would be made. My father was so conscious of the fact that war was going to happen that he had already had an air raid shelter built within the garage of our house. It was like something on the Maginot Line, built entirely of concrete, that my dad arranged to be built after the Munich Crisis. (The Maginot Line was a series of concrete fortifications built by the French as a defence against Germany.) The first time we went into the shelter we realised that it was at such a low level that there was six inches of water in it. The shelter was full of frogs and we never ever used it.

We listened with anticipation for the announcement of the war taking place. Within a short while of having heard Neville Chamberlain there was an air raid warning. The sound of the siren, for a short time, produced chaos where we lived. People thought it was an actual air raid but eventually they realised it was safe.

At the start of the war I was an apprentice engineer at North Walbottle Colliery in Northumberland. My father and other family members were colliery engineers and in those days you followed the traditional occupation. I had started the year before when I was fourteen. My apprentice wage was 9 shillings and sixpence (47$\frac{1}{2}$ pence). My working hours were 7 am to 4 pm – Monday to Friday (with $\frac{1}{2}$ hour for lunch) and 6 am to 12 pm on a Saturday. If you were five minutes late for work you were docked a $\frac{1}{4}$ of a shift's pay.

North Walbottle Colliery before the Second World War.

I had not been at the colliery very long when the person in charge said: 'Well, you have to be initiated sometime.' There had been a breakdown on the coal face underground. He said, 'You'll have to carry my kit,' – it was a shoulder bag with all the equipment in. We went underground and the person at the bottom of the shaft was a man called Tom Severs, the son of the original colliery manager, who said to me: 'Well lad, this is your first day in the pit. You have to have a chow.' I didn't know what a chow was. He took out a block of Warhorse Tobacco and then with a knife cut a wad off and said: 'That's your chow.' I then put it in my mouth and chewed and off we went. We were underground a long time as it was a good walk to the coal face and then the repairs had to be done. As we came out the person I was with said: 'By the way Tom, I haven't seen you spitting the tobacco juice out.'

I said: 'I didn't know I was supposed to spit it out!' Throughout all that time underground I had been swallowing the juice produced by chewing the tobacco. I blame that day for me having a bad stomach ever since.

The war was brought into our lives at close quarters when a German bomber crashed at the nearby village of Westerhope in May 1941. The plane was a Heinkel 3 that was returning from a bombing mission at Glasgow. On its return journey it was intercepted and brought down by one of our fighters. It was quite a dramatic experience for local people because one of the crew tried to jump out of the plane before it landed and was killed instantly. The rest of the crew survived and the pilot attempted to blow up the plane with a bomb they were carrying. He was prevented from doing so by the many people who arrived at the scene and ensured he couldn't detonate the bomb. A number of Westerhope Home Guard personnel were there and they took the crew to the nearby miners' institute where they were held and attempts were made to get them to confess what they had been doing. There was some humour in the situation when it was noticed that a member of the Home Guard was in full uniform but still had his carpet slippers on!

The crashed Heinkel at Westerhope in May 1941.

There was a tragic incident in North Walbottle when one night there was an air raid on Tyneside. The planes were targeting the Vickers-Armstrong factory by the river but it was a cloudy night and couldn't locate it. Bombs fell on North Walbottle instead and three local people were killed – a train driver, his daughter and their neighbour. The train driver's daughter was due to be married within a few days and her wedding dress was hanging on the pantry door.

One of the precautions for bombing raids was to put brown tape on your window to prevent glass blowing into your house if a bomb dropped nearby. The black-out was enforced by the ARP wardens and people were quickly alerted if there was any light showing from your house. I can't recall any one being prosecuted if they didn't obey the black-out instructions. One experience of my wife's family was when she lived in Low Fell and her brother worked on night shift. He came home one night and left a light on that could be seen. A warden from Whickham – which is quite a distance away – came over to Low Fell to tell them of the fact the light was blazing out. Luckily, they weren't prosecuted for it.

I was at North Walbottle pit for fifteen months but I had an uncle who was chief engineer at Choppington Colliery, near Bedlington, and he wanted to take me on and progress me as a young engineer. During the time I was at Choppington a man came to see my uncle. He was about to go in my uncle's office and I said excuse me you need an introduction so I took this man's card. I went into see my uncle who said: 'Send him in, Tom.' The man was called Hugh Wood and he was the owner of a mining machinery company. The next time he came to see my uncle he said: 'If you want a job you can come to Team Valley to work for me.' So in 1941 I left Choppington and joined Hugh Wood and Company in Team Valley and I was there for 46 years.

While at Hugh Wood's I joined the Home Guard and also took part in fire watching. There were lots of incendiary bombs dropped in the area but we were never confronted with any at Team Valley. There was about eight of us who used to have to fire watch and we stayed overnight at the factory. We took it in turns to look out and then tried to get some sleep. Then we went straight to work. At this time I was trained to use a stirrup pump to put out any fires caused by incendiary bombs.

As well as fire watching we trained twice a week with the Home Guard – particularly on a Sunday morning. I was going to evening classes Monday, Wednesday and Friday and I was courting at the time. Then on Tuesday evening I started training at St James' Park.

I was playing inside right for Westerhope Juniors and we had outstanding team. People used to come and watch and someone recommended I apply for a trial with Newcastle United. I was nineteen years old at the time. I had three trials and, at the end of the third trial, the Newcastle director Stan Seymour senior said he would like to sign me on amateur forms. In each trial I had scored so that must have impressed Seymour. I was signed with two other players who were Charlie Crowe and Ernie Taylor and we were paraded into the directors' room. It was an absolutely tremendous occasion for me. I remember Ernie Taylor was wearing his navy uniform. He looked too small to be a footballer and I thought if he can make it so can I. But, despite his size, he was an outstanding footballer who went on to play for Newcastle for several years, including the 1951 FA Cup Final. He then moved on to Blackpool and played in the famous Stanley Matthews' Cup Final of 1953 – again Ernie was on the winning side. Further clubs included Manchester United and Sunderland (his hometown club). Charlie Crowe also played in the 1951 Final and stayed with United for many years. After he retired he wrote two successful books – one of them was called 'A Crowe Amongst the Magpies'. The books were sold for local charities.

Newcastle United's Charlie Crowe with goalkeeper Ronnie Simpson.

So on Tuesday evenings I was training at St James' Park. Training was primitive in those days and we wore heavy jerseys and shorts. We didn't think about it at the time but we were using the same kit that people had been wearing for weeks. I don't know when it was ever washed. I was on the books at Newcastle for two years but I was not to have the glittering career of the men I signed on with – Charlie Crowe and Ernie Taylor.

While I was working at Hugh Wood's I volunteered for the RAF aircrew but my application was rejected because I worked for a company which was under the Essential Works Order. My job was seen as a reserved occupation and I couldn't leave to join the Forces. My brother worked for the same company and my mother was virtually ostracised by members of the village because she had two sons at home while the rest of the village lads were in the Armed Forces. It was something that I always resented. I thought we should have had a badge to show the fact that we were on Essential Works Order. This could have eliminated some of the embarrassment my parents and I had.

It was after the war, in 1950, that I got married. Clothing rationing was still in place and for months my wife bought coupons from people so she would have enough for her wedding outfit. Just before we were to be married, clothes came off the ration and she had wasted her money buying the coupons. As for wedding cakes, in order to make sure you had a cake you had to register with three different people because there was no guarantee they could make you one in time. So you could easily end up with two or three different cakes. One of our most embarrassing experiences of married life was when we went to the Isle of Man for our honeymoon. My wife's ration book was still in her maiden name and you could imagine the embarrassment when we handed the receptionist her ration book which you had to do when you stayed somewhere. The receptionist thought we weren't married.

Whenever I say to someone that I am from Westerhope, if that person is of a certain age, they will mention Harris's Gardens on Stamfordham Road. So many people I meet remember joining long queues for tomatoes from Harris's. These queues could reach 150 yards long such was the demand for their tomatoes. But that was how it was during the war.

Tom Peacock (wearing the jacket) while youth hostelling with workers from Hugh Wood's factory in 1944.

Women at War

Left: Members of Brandon WVS, at Langley Moor, completing their civil defence training.

The Women's Volunteer Service (WVS) was founded in 1938 and its motto was 'The WVS Never Says No.' Over one million women volunteered for service and their duties included everything from civil defence to knitting clothes as well as running mobile canteens and helping bombed-out families. Other women joined the Royal Navy (WRNS); the RAF (WAAF); the Women's Auxiliary Fire Service and the Auxiliary Territorial Services (ATS). One member of the ATS was Elizabeth Windsor – the future Queen.

Left: A Women's Voluntary Services mobile canteen at Ashfield House, Joicey Road, Gateshead. The plaque on the vehicle reads: 'Presented by the American Red Cross in memory of Percy Chubb. A friend of Britain.'

A group of Land Army Girls clearing scrubland near Darlington after the war. Over 80,000 women worked on the land to help keep Britain fed.

Above: Women who were employed at Shildon Railway Works in 1943. At this time almost eight million women were employed in war work.

In County Durham over 15,000 women worked at the Royal Ordnance factory in Aycliffe. They were known as the Aycliffe Angels – a name given to them by Lord Haw-Haw, the notorious radio broadcaster of German propaganda. He said: 'the little angels of Aycliffe will not get away with it.'

Assembling ammunition is a dangerous job and a number of women were killed in accidents.

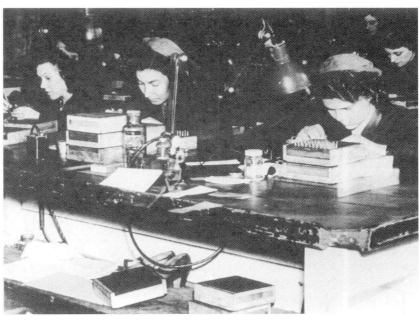

Above: Miss A. Lynn, Miss E. Saunders and Miss H. May who were solderers in the Vickers-Armstrong Works, Newcastle.

Left: The smiling faces of workers making shells at Vickers-Armstrong during the Second World War. Why are the flags flying? Was it a time for celebrating or was there an important visitor to the works?

Women also worked in the shipyards on the Tyne and Wear helping to build the ships that were vital to the war effort.

Almost Shot by the Air Force
by Jack Hair

I was born on 2nd April 1939 at 31 Joicey Square, Stanley and was the youngest of three children to Billy and Isa Hair. This was five months before the outbreak of the Second World War. These old houses in Joicey Square were some of the first houses built in Stanley and were very basic indeed. The ceilings in the downstairs rooms had exposed wooden beams and my mother decided to cover them with wallpaper to give them the effect of a level ceiling. Apparently, soon after, they were awakened in the night with a terrible scratching sound. On investigation, they discovered this unearthly noise was coming from within the wall-papered beams. On removal of a length of the paper, dozens of black beetles cascaded down on to the kitchen floor. We soon moved from that house.

Jack Hair.

At this time my father worked at Beamish Mary Colliery and we were allocated a house at 4 Railway Terrace, Shield Row, which was a tied house. Tied houses were houses belonging to the colliery, allocated only to their workers and dependant on employment at their collieries.

When the war started we had an Anderson Shelter erected in the front garden. This shelter, named after one of the wartime Ministers, was supposed to give protection against German bombers and was comprised of semi-circular tin sheets built in the form of a shed, partly below ground level and covered over with soil and grass turf. Every time the air raid siren sounded we would go into the shelter until the all clear siren was sounded. Sometimes we were in the shelter for many hours.

Just behind Railway Terrace was the rail line from Newcastle to Consett and there were regular wagons fitted with anti-aircraft guns to protect them from enemy planes. We lived only fifty or so yards from Shield Row Station. After many weeks and months of going in and out of the shelter due to threatened air attack, my parents were exhausted for lack of sleep and decided that no matter what happened we were all going to stay in our own beds in the house. The next morning my mother went to George Rainbow's shop opposite Shield Row Post Office. While being served, others in the shop were talking of the bombs that had dropped at Beamish during the night.

The Auxiliary Fire Service in Stanley during the Second World War. Included in the picture: Mr Knox, Joseph Hall, Mr Traverse, Mr Pounder and Andrew Moore (chief).

Well, as you could imagine, my mother was quite shocked as Beamish was only one mile down the railway line from Shield Row. As the result of that bomb raid, eight people lost their lives and many others were seriously injured.

Not long after that we, as a family, had been to my grandparents house in Wylam Road and were making our way back to Railway Terrace. Suddenly, as we passed the park, a German bomber passed overhead and was being chased by a British fighter which was doing its best to shoot down the enemy plane. The fighter was shooting at him with his machine guns and the tracer bullets were hitting the ground around us and we were very lucky not to be killed. Imagine, almost being shot by our own air force in your own streets.

Other early memories, although not particularly in year order, are of the end of the war. There were huge celebrations with the bonfire of all bonfires on the Store Field. Placed on top of this huge bonfire were stuffed dummies with the faces of Hitler and his generals such as, Goebbels, Goering and the Italian leader, Mussolini. There were speeches, street parties and firework displays. Soon, large numbers of the armed forces were returning home to great celebration, united once again with their loved ones. Some children had not seen their fathers during the entire war. Sadly, some of them did not return home, killed defending their country in some far off distant land. For these families there was only great heartache.

Gone was the sound of the air raid warning siren. No more telegrams informing of 'Missing, believed dead'. No more foreign soldiers based in the area. All that was left to remind us of the war were the air raid shelters erected in people's back gardens and yards.

The other main thing was the great shortage of food and many other household items. Rationing had been in place for many years. Some items of food began re-appearing in the shops. For example,

A Victory in Europe Party in Joicey Square, Stanley in 1945.

I had never seen a banana before. Dried egg powder was the normal thing to use for baking. Even coal was rationed. Our family did not seem to go without much. My parents were great providers, although I sometimes believe they went without to make sure we had food.

One of the great shortages was cigarettes and I often walked the streets with friends looking for cigarette ends in the gutters so they could take them home for their fathers to re-roll their own makeshift cigarettes. This may now seem disgusting, but these were desperate times for smokers. Luckily, my parents did not smoke.

It was long after the war before things returned to normal and if any of the shops got supplies of either cigarettes or sweets, news would spread around the town like wildfire and long queues would soon appear. When these rare supplies ran out, there were often ugly scenes of men demonstrating their great dissatisfaction and, sometimes, the police would be called in to disperse the crowds. I remember the Ministry of Food had an office at the top of our street at Clifford Road from where the ration books were distributed. One coupon of each entitled you to a measured amount.

One man in our back street who always seemed to have a few sweets for the kids was George Batty of Lucy Street. He kept pigs, livestock and poultry on his allotment garden. It was the normal thing for neighbours to keep any waste food and vegetable peelings to help George feed his animals. When we, as children, took him these supplies he would always give you a couple of Mint Imperial sweets. George also kept other animals such as ferrets and rabbits. His ferrets were kept to kill off rats and other vermin on the heaps behind the Fire Station. Often as kids, we would wait with him for hours until the ferrets came out of the holes in the heaps. Vegetables seemed plentiful as allotment gardens sprang up on any unused piece of land. The slogan was 'Dig For Victory'.

Helping With The War Effort

Right: An advert from a Theatre Royal programme giving the amount collected for a 'Spitfire Fund'. Howard & Wyndham were the owners of a number of theatres, including the Theatre Royal in Newcastle.

Fund-raising played an important part in the war effort. Not only did it raise money but it also boosted morale and helped people feel like they were 'doing their bit'. Raising money for Spitfires was very popular amongst companies and communities.

HOWARD & WYNDHAM SPITFIRE FUND.

FUND TO DATE totals

£975 18s. 8d.

GO TO IT ! KEEP AT IT ! !

and " ROLL OUT YOUR SAVINGS " for this Fund.

THANK YOU !

A Spitfire at an air show at Usworth Airfield after the war.

What British Planes Cost

A Tyneside newspaper in August 1940 gave these figures for the costs of aeroplanes:

Spitfire	£6,000
Hurricane	£4,500
Blenheim	£17,000
Wellington	£25,000
Sunderland	£50,000

The Spitfire and the Hurricane were the famous planes that helped win the Battle of Britain. The Blenheim and the Wellington were bombers while the Sunderland was a sea plane used for attacking enemy submarines.

Above: T.H. White of Shildon won prizes at various carnivals during the Second World War years impersonating Hitler. He is holding a collecting tin and donations were given to charities.

Left: A crashed Messerschmitt was put on display in the North East in 1940 to raise money for a Spitfire Fund. Here Home Guard troops and some civilians inspect the wreckage. One young lad is sitting in the remains of the cockpit.

Other fundraising campaigns included: War Weapons Week; Salute the Soldier Week; Warship Week; Tank Week and 'Wings For Victory Week – Salute to the RAF'.

Right: Children collecting scrap metal in Hetton, County Durham, around 1940. Around this time there was a major campaign to collect as much metal as possible. These youngsters have pans, dustbin lids, buckets, a pram frame and tin baths. The most visible result of the metal drive was the loss of iron railings around parks and gardens. However, not all this scrap was suitable for the purpose it was collected for – building ships, aircraft and tanks.

Fund raising for the war-effort on Stanley Front Street in 1942. The pavement is packed with people watching the band leading the troops. Most of the men are wearing flat caps while young lads in balaclavas walk alongside the troops.

Three Bangs Meant the 'All Clear'
by Evan Martin

In 1938 my dad got a deputy's job at Bomarsund Colliery near Bedlington. A colliery house was his at the Bomar (geographically Stakeford, but the houses were inhabited by Bomarsund miners). I became so attached to that house in West Terrace, next to Eliza and Tom Smailes, that when Dad had the chance of a bigger house in the pit yard (Office Houses) I didn't sleep for a week worrying in case we had to move (all of 200 yards). We thankfully stayed, and the Martins occupied 51 West Terrace for fifty-three years. My mother lived in the same house for 62 years. One of her neighbours lived next door for 58 years – the other next door neighbour was there for 48 years. We all grew up together and lived through hard times such as the Second World War.

Summer days were often spent at the seaside. Cambois was a walk away along the colliery line. Blyth could be reached by the 41 bus every half hour and I loved Newbiggin best because of the 'willicks' that were bought on the Front Street, Fisher End. None of those places on a fine summer's day I remember as clearly as one day in early September 1939.

We arrived at South Shields via the 42 bus to North Shields, the ferry across and the walk down Ocean Road. I can recall sitting on the beach and a local man telling my father something which disturbed him and meant our packing up and leaving for home. I understood years later that it was that day Neville Chamberlain had announced we were at war with Hitler's Germany.

During the war years, Dad was often on ARP duty at nights. My mother wasn't aware of air raid warnings because of her hearing loss and neighbours, Mrs Lake on one side and Eliza on the other, banged twice on the walls to warn us of potential bombing. This inspired us to take to the safety of the 'dark hole', a cupboard under the stairs, where Mam had a deck chair and I a makeshift bed. Three bangs meant the 'all clear' had gone and we were back to normal.

A bomb dropped in the fields behind the allotments around 1943. We were told it hadn't gone off, but it certainly rattled the windows and caused much diving under kitchen tables, with the impact recoil.

The war years meant total black-out in the rows. Even the 100 watt colliery street lamp was doused at Eliza's corner. My big pal at the time was Billy Wilkin. One night he'll not forget was when he was four and I was three. He lived at 49 East Terrace almost opposite our 51 West. Often Billy popped across for company and this

Evan Martin when he was a boy and sixty years later.

particular winter's evening he'd played with my soldiers and fort (made by Mr Hopper at 48 West Terrace) and helped himself, as I had, to Mam's plateful of store raisins. Seven o'clock came and Mam opened the back door to let Billy out and across the lane. I decided the raisins had worked too well and Mam quickly provided a bucket which was thankfully used and carried over the yard to the netty, where unknown to anyone, Billy was sitting; he also having been taken short by the raisin attack.

Mother didn't see him and he was covered by the bucketful and nearly flushed away as she, in one movement, tipped the pail and pulled the chain. Billy, according to Dad who was at the back door, moaned with an extended 'Ugh', which just about summed up his feelings. My mother washed Billy's clothes and Mrs Wilkin saw the funny side of the situation.

A treat would be fish and chips from Coxon's Chip Shop. We usually had a long wait as it seemed Mr Coxon cooked one order at a time. Mrs Coxon kept us kids entertained by giving us words to spell. The winner getting a couple of chips. During the war, paper was difficult to collect due to the war effort. Fish and chips were put straight on to the newsprint of the paper – no finery such as greaseproof pieces in those days.

At one time, Mrs Coxon was short of newspaper and said she would give a free bag of chips to anyone bringing ten sheets of paper to the shop. Some of the streets' bright sparks had the notion of pinching newspapers from the back of the street lavatory cistern pipes. Mrs Coxon soon caught on and they were chased.

Victory Celebrations

Victory in Europe Day was celebrated on 8th May 1945. On that day Winston Churchill gave the following speech:

'This is your victory! It is the victory of the cause of freedom in every land. In all our long history we have never seen a greater day than this. Everyone, man or woman, has done their best. Everyone has tried. Neither the long years, nor the dangers, nor the fierce attacks of the enemy, have in any way weakened the independent resolve of the British nation.'

Right: Prime Minister Winston Churchill with his wife Clementine.

Below: A VE Party at Granby Buildings, Morpeth. Thick-cut slices of bread and home-made cakes are on the table.

Parties like this were held in every part of the country. Many in the North East took place in the back lanes between streets. Tables, chairs and white table cloths came out of everyone's home. Decorations were quickly made or old pre-war bunting from perhaps the King's Coronation of 1937 was put up in the streets and Union Jacks were prominent. Food was still rationed but families shared what they had to provide a celebratory tea.

Right: Residents of Maria Street and Maughan Street, Benwell, gather in their back lane on VE Day. Some of the women on the left are giving the 'V for Victory' sign made famous by Churchill.

Here are three photos of a VE Party in Tamworth Road, Arthur's Hill, Newcastle. Wounded soldiers from the nearby General Hospital were invited to join the party. Although Britain was celebrating there was still fighting in the Far East. Japan was not to surrender for another three months.

Right: Two soldiers with eye injuries cut the cake on VE Day.

Left: Dancing in Tamworth Road on VE Day. With not enough men to go around, two women on the left dance with each other.

Below: The wounded soldiers, arm in arm with the Newcastle lasses, enjoy the end of the war in Europe.

Right: Members of the Home Guard and the local colliery band at Tantobie, near Stanley, after the war ended. At the front is an effigy with a swastika, perhaps to go on one of the many bonfires that were lit that night.

Left: ARP Wardens marching along Regent Street, Blyth, during a Victory Parade in 1945. Note the badges on their uniforms 'CD' for Civil Defence. Men such as these, who volunteered for many hours of service, could now return to a normal life

Right: A victory parade at St James' Park, Newcastle in May 1945. Service men and women are on the pitch, dignitaries in the main stand with the public standing on the terraces. A Victory Concert was also held at Newcastle's City Hall on VE Day.

Acknowledgements

The author would like to thank the following who have kindly helped with this book:

Geoffrey Berriman, Steve Boundey, Alan Brett, Maisie Tait Cuthbertson, Anne Dixon, George Forster, Peter Gibson, Ron Handley, Eileen Hopper, George and Phyllis Laws, Jim Pace, Tom Peacock, Don Price, Brian Scott, Neil Taylor, Sharyn Taylor, Norma Thompson, Lorna Windham, Jim Windham and Yvonne Young.

Beamish Museum – The Living Museum of the North
North Tyneside Libraries
West Newcastle Picture History Collection

Ann Nora Robinson's story 'Gas Masks and Gun Fire' was first published in *Women of Old County Durham* by Margaret McReady

Brian Scott's story 'Air Raid Shelters and Schooldays' was first published in *Southwick* by Peter Gibson

Maisie Tait Cuthbertson's story 'Parachute Mine and Prayers' was first published in *Lynemouth* by Neil Taylor

George Forster's story 'Watching the Battle of Britain' was first published in *Seaham Then & Now* by George Hoare & Ian Wright

Evan Martin's story 'Three Bangs Meant The All Clear' was first published in *Memories of Bedlington and Beyond* by Evan Martin

Bibliography

County Durham & Northumberland During The Second World War by Geoffrey Berriman
Durham Bairns by Andrew Clark & Anne Dixon
Newbiggin by the Sea by Mike Kirkup
Sunderland Blitz by Kevin Brady
Tyneside at War by Clive Hardy & Paul Harris
War on the Home Front by Juliet Gardiner
Westerhope Remembered by Tom Peacock & Ron Handley

Evening Chronicle
Sunderland Echo
The War Illustrated

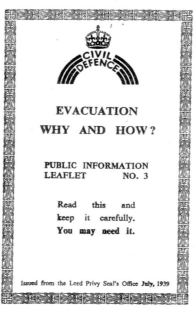

A 1943 Garden Seeds catalogue from Thomas Matheson & Son, Morpeth, that encouraged you to 'Grow More Vegetables'.

A public information leaflet for 'Evacuation Why and How?'

The front cover of a leaflet for the famous 'Dig For Victory' campaign.

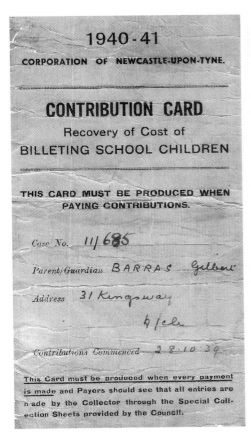

Above: The author's collection of gas masks. At the far left is a child's respirator, the so called 'Mickey Mouse' gas mask that was coloured red and blue to make it more attractive for youngsters. In the middle and right are two adult respirators and at the back is a baby's helmet.

Left: A contribution card for recovering the cost of billeting an evacuee from Newcastle.

Above: The Souvenir Programme for Newcastle's Victory Celebrations in 1946. A Parade was held on 8th June and a Tattoo at the City Hall on the 8th, 9th & 10th June.

Right: Arthur Dykes' wartime pass allowing him to enter Laing's Shipyard, Sunderland.

A wartime helmet. Millions of these were made during the war and were often worn by civilian uniformed service personal. Helmets would have the letter 'W' on them for Warden – 'AFS' for the Auxiliary Fire Service' – or 'DC' for decontamination squad.

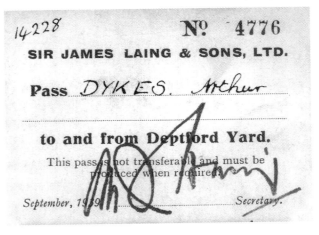

Also available from Summerhill Books

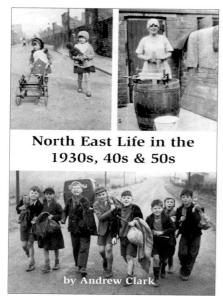

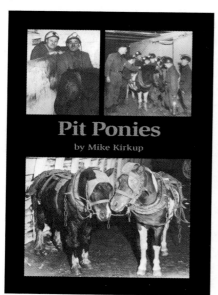

North East Life in the 1930s, 40s & 50s

by Andrew Clark

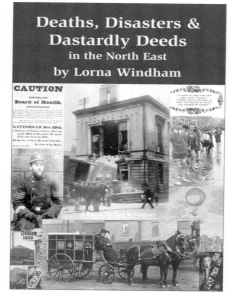

Deaths, Disasters & Dastardly Deeds
in the North East
by Lorna Windham

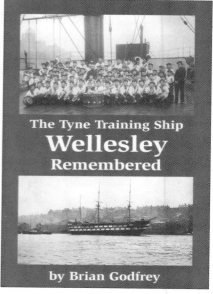

The Tyne Training Ship Wellesley Remembered

by Brian Godfrey

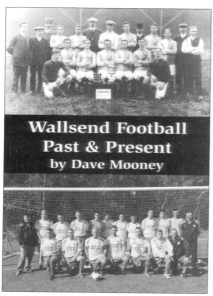

Wallsend Football Past & Present
by Dave Mooney

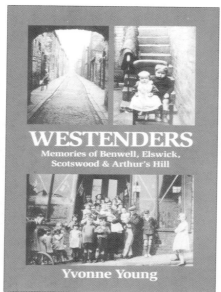

WESTENDERS
Memories of Benwell, Elswick, Scotswood & Arthur's Hill

Yvonne Young

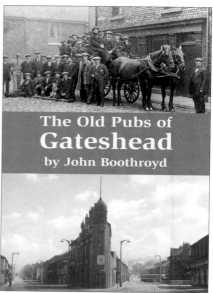

The Old Pubs of Gateshead
by John Boothroyd

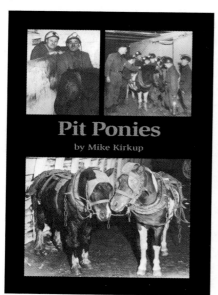

Pit Ponies
by Mike Kirkup

Backworth Remembered

by Robert Mitchelson

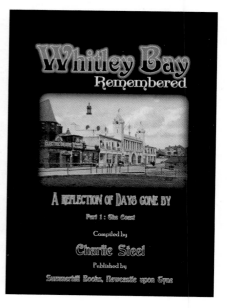

Whitley Bay Remembered

A REFLECTION OF DAYS GONE BY

Part 1: The Coast

Compiled by
Charlie Steel

Published by
Summerhill Books, Newcastle upon Tyne

visit our website to view our full range of books
www.summerhillbooks.co.uk